CONTINENTS

North America

Mary Virginia Fox

Heinemann
LIBRARY

H www.heinemann.co.uk/library

Visit our website to find out more information about Heinemann Library books.

To order:

☎ Phone 44 (0) 1865 888066

Send a fax to 44 (0) 1865 314091

Visit the Heinemann Bookshop at www.heinemann.co.uk/library to browse our catalogue and order online.

First published in Great Britain by Heinemann Library, Halley Court, Jordan Hill, Oxford OX2 8EJ, part of Harcourt Education. Heinemann is a registered trademark of Harcourt Education Ltd.

© Harcourt Education Ltd 2002, 2006
First published in paperback in 2007
The moral right of the proprietor has been asserted.

Editorial: Kathy Peltan, Cla~
Design: Joanna Hinton-Ma~
Picture research: Erica Ne~
Production: Helen McCrea~

Origination: Modern Age Repro House Ltd.
Printed and bound in China by South China Printing Co. Ltd.

13-digit ISBN 978-0-431-15807-5 (hardback)
10 09 08 07 06
10 9 8 7 6 5 4 3 2 1

13-digit ISBN 978-0-431-09896-8 (paperback)
11 10 09 08 07
10 9 8 7 6 5 4 3 2 1

British Library Cataloguing in Publication Data

Fox, Mary Virginia
North America. – 2nd ed. – (Continents)
917
A full catalogue record for this book is available from the British Library.

Acknowledgements

The ~~~~ 'ishers would like to thank the following for permission ~~~~ ~duce photographs: Getty Images/Robert Harding World ~~~/R H Productions, 5, Bruce Coleman, Inc./Dr. Eckart Pott, ~th Scenes/S. Osolinski, p. 9; Bruce Coleman, Inc./Bob ~ 11; Corbis/Scott T. Smith, p. 13; Bruce Coleman, ~. Fogden, p. 14; Bruce Coleman, Inc./Ed Degginger, p. ~e Coleman, Inc./Peter French, p. 16; Bruce Coleman, ~ Gunnar, p. 17; Bruce Coleman, Inc./J. Sarapochiello, ~ny Stone/Joseph Pobereskin, p. 21; Bruce Coleman, ~on Smith, p. 22; Tony Stone/Donald Nausbaum, p. 23; ~enes/Eastcott/Momotiak/p. 24; Bruce Coleman, Inc./ ~on, p. 25; Photo Edit/Myrleen Ferguson, p. 27; Tony Stone/Doug Armand, p. 28; Photo Edit/Cindy Charles, p. 29.

Cover photograph of North America, reproduced with permission of Science Photo Library/ Tom Van Sant, Geosphere Project/ Planetary Visions.

The publishers would like to thank Kathy Peltan, Keith Lye, and Nancy Harris for their assistance in the preparation of this book.

Every effort has been made to contact copyright holders of any material reproduced in this book. Any omissions will be rectified in subsequent printings if notice is given to the publishers.

Some words are shown in bold, **like this**. You can find out what they mean by looking in the glossary.

Contents

Where is North America?

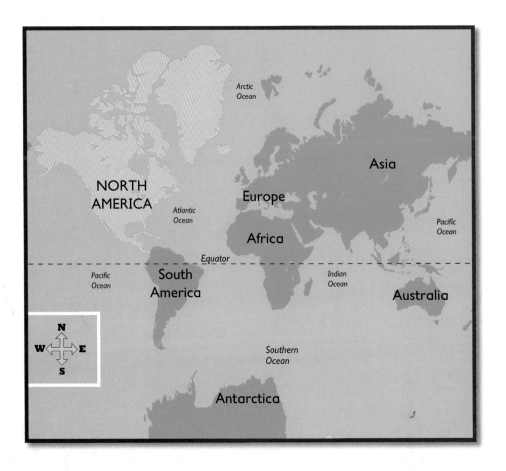

There are seven continents. A continent is a very large area of land. North America is the third largest continent. It stretches north beyond the **Arctic Circle**. In the south, a narrow strip of land connects North and South America.

On either side of North America, there are two great oceans. To the west is the Pacific Ocean. To the east is the Atlantic Ocean. North America includes many islands. Some of these islands belong to countries that are in other continents.

Greenland is part of the continent of North America, but it belongs to Denmark, in Europe.

▲ *The large island of Greenland in the Arctic Ocean*

Weather

North America has many different **climates**. In the south, the weather is very warm, and it often rains. In the south west, there are hot **deserts**. Along the west coast, the sun shines most of the time.

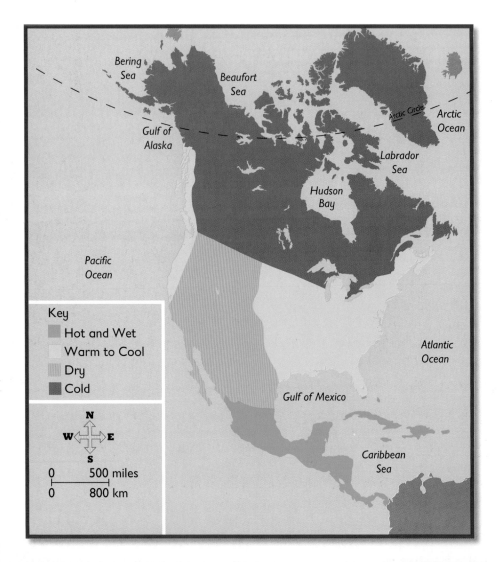

Bering Sea

Beaufort Sea

Arctic Circle

Arctic Ocean

Gulf of Alaska

Labrador Sea

Hudson Bay

Pacific Ocean

Atlantic Ocean

Gulf of Mexico

Caribbean Sea

Key
- Hot and Wet
- Warm to Cool
- Dry
- Cold

N
W
E
S

| 0 | 500 miles |
| 0 | 800 km |

▲ *Frozen ground in northern Canada*

Near the **Arctic Circle**, the ground stays frozen all year. The northwest coast is cool and rainy. But in much of North America, it is cold and snowy in winter, and hot in summer.

Mountains and deserts

There are high mountain **ranges** along the west of North America. The Rocky Mountains go from the **deserts** of Mexico to icy Alaska. The Appalachian Mountains in the east are older and lower than the Rocky Mountains.

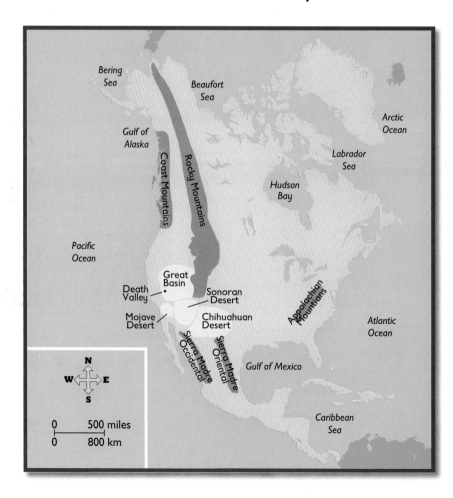

This dry, stony desert is hot in the day and cold at night.

▲ *Sonoran Desert, New Mexico, USA*

There are several large deserts in the southwest United States and Mexico. Death Valley is a desert in California. It is the hottest place in the United States. The temperature there has reached 57°C (135°F).

Rivers

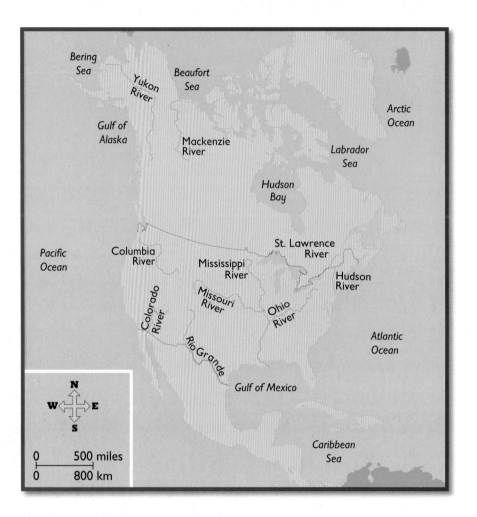

The Mississippi is one of the world's most important rivers. It starts near the Canadian **border**. It then flows south through the centre of the United States. Two other great rivers, the Missouri and the Ohio, run into the Mississippi.

The St Lawrence River runs eastwards from the Great Lakes to the Atlantic Ocean. Large ocean-going ships can travel along the river because **canals** take ships safely from one place to another.

▲ *Canal on the St Lawrence River*

Lakes

There are five large **freshwater** lakes close to the **border** of the USA and Canada. They are called the Great Lakes. The lakes are linked to each other by **canals**, so large ships can travel between them.

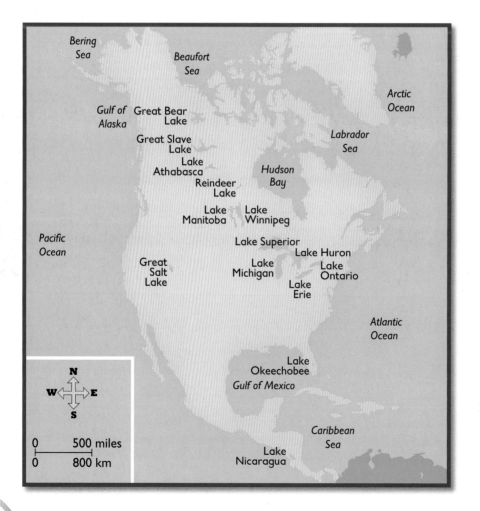

Bering Sea

Beaufort Sea

Arctic Ocean

Gulf of Alaska

Great Bear Lake

Labrador Sea

Great Slave Lake

Lake Athabasca

Hudson Bay

Reindeer Lake

Lake Manitoba

Lake Winnipeg

Pacific Ocean

Lake Superior

Lake Huron

Great Salt Lake

Lake Michigan

Lake Ontario

Lake Erie

Atlantic Ocean

Lake Okeechobee

Gulf of Mexico

N
W   E
S

0   500 miles
0   800 km

Caribbean Sea

Lake Nicaragua

▲ *Great Salt Lake, Utah, USA*

The Great Salt Lake is a **shallow** lake in a **desert**. It is in the west of North America. Its water is very salty. Swimmers can easily float in it.

Animals

Millions of bison, also called buffalo, used to live on the grassy **plains** of North America. Golden eagles and pumas live in the mountains of the north. Alligators and turtles lurk in the **swamps** of Florida, in the south.

▼ *Bison in a national park, South Dakota, USA*

Most bison live in **national parks**, to protect them from hunters.

▲ *Polar bear in the Arctic*

Polar bears live in the frozen north of the continent. They hunt for fish where there are breaks in the ice. Whales, walruses, and seals swim in the icy Arctic Sea.

Plants

Redwoods are the tallest trees in the world. Some grow to 112 metres (367 feet) tall.

▲ Redwood trees, California, USA

Giant redwood trees grow on the northwest coast of the United States. Maple trees grow in Canada and the northeast of the United States. In spring, people use the **sap** from inside the trees to make **maple syrup**.

Many types of cactus grow in the **deserts** of the south west. Saguaro cactuses are very tough. They need very little water to survive.

Saguaro cactuses can be as tall as a four-storey building.

▲ *Saguaro cactuses, Mexico*

Languages

The first people living in North America were **Native Americans**. They had their own languages. Now only a few Native Americans use these languages. Most people in the United States speak English. There are also many people who speak Spanish.

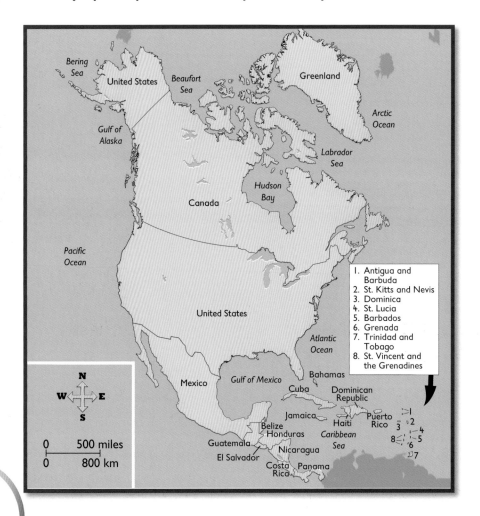

1. Antigua and Barbuda
2. St. Kitts and Nevis
3. Dominica
4. St. Lucia
5. Barbados
6. Grenada
7. Trinidad and Tobago
8. St. Vincent and the Grenadines

▲ Oaxaca City, Mexico

The area south of the United States is called Central America. Most people in Central America speak Spanish. In Canada, some people speak French.

Cities

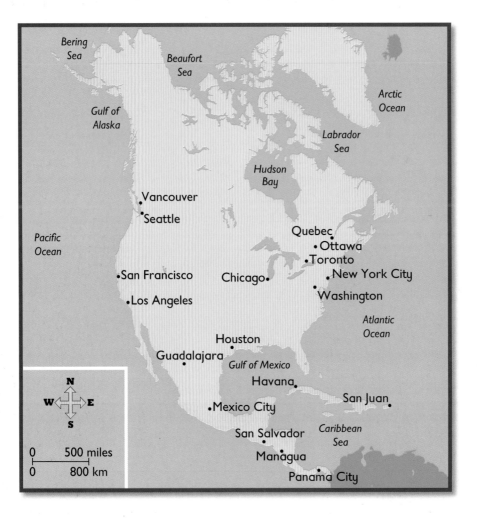

This map shows some of the main cities in the continent of North America. Toronto, in Canada, is a busy **port** on Lake Ontario. Ottawa is the **capital city** of Canada. The Canadian **parliament** meets there.

New York City is one of the most important cities in the world. People from all over the world visit the city for business and fun. New York City is famous for its tall skyscrapers.

▲ *Skyscrapers in New York City*

Mexico City is the largest city in North America. It is an important business centre. It has many modern buildings. It also has lots of churches built by Spanish **settlers**.

The ruins of an ancient city, built by the **Aztecs**, lie under Mexico City.

▲ *Mexico City, Mexico*

Havana was built by Spanish settlers about 500 years ago.

▲ Havana, Cuba

Havana is the **capital city** of Cuba. Cuba is the biggest island in the Caribbean Sea. Havana is a lively centre for jazz musicians and singers. It sells cigars, sugar, coffee, and fruit to other countries.

In the country

▲ *Harvesting wheat in Alberta, Canada*

North America has many types of countryside.
In the centre are **plains** covered with wheat
fields. Near the coasts, farmers raise cattle. In
forests in Canada, **lumberjacks** cut down
trees and saw them into logs.

On the northeast coast, people go fishing for cod and mackerel. In the countries around the Caribbean Sea, the **climate** is good for growing coffee, sugar, and bananas.

▲ *Picking bananas in Costa Rica*

Famous places

Yellowstone Park is the oldest **national park** in the world. The park contains hundreds of geysers. Geysers are jets of hot steam that shoot up suddenly out of the ground.

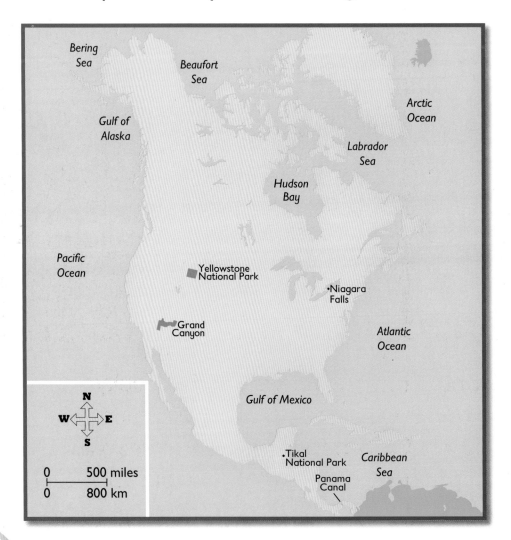

Bering Sea

Beaufort Sea

Arctic Ocean

Gulf of Alaska

Labrador Sea

Hudson Bay

Pacific Ocean

Yellowstone National Park

•Niagara Falls

•Grand Canyon

Atlantic Ocean

Gulf of Mexico

N
W E
S

0   500 miles
0   800 km

•Tikal National Park

Caribbean Sea

Panama Canal

The Grand Canyon is 446 km (277 miles) long.

▲ *Grand Canyon, Arizona, USA*

The Grand Canyon is a very steep, rocky river valley. It was formed over millions of years by the Colorado River. The river water cut through the layers of rock to make this deep canyon.

Niagara Falls forms part of the **border** between the United States and Canada.

▲ *Niagara Falls, Ontario, Canada*

Niagara Falls is made up of two big waterfalls. The American Falls are in the United States. The Horseshoe Falls are in Canada. Boats take visitors close to the crashing water.

The Maya people lived in Central America about 800 years ago. They built stone cities in forests. At the centre of these cities were **temples** shaped like pyramids.

The Maya people had their own way of writing. They used picture symbols.

▲ *Mayan pyramid, Tikal, Guatemala*

Fast facts

Longest rivers in North America

Name of river	Length in Kilometres	Length in miles	Begins	Ends
Missouri	4,087	2,540	Rocky Mountains	Mississippi River
Mississippi	3,781	2,350	Minnesota	Gulf of Mexico
Yukon	3,184	1,979	Canada	Bering Sea

Highest mountains in major mountain ranges in North America

Name of mountain	Range	Height in metres	Height in feet	Country or US State
Mt McKinley	Alaska Range	6,194	20,320	Alaska
Mt Whitney	Sierra Nevada	4,418	14,494	California
Mt Elbert	Rocky Mountains	4,401	14,439	Colorado

North America's record-breakers

The **border** between Canada and the USA is the world's longest land border.
Lake Superior on the border of Canada and the USA is the world's largest **freshwater** lake.
The Great Salt Lake in Utah is saltier than the oceans.
The Mississippi, Missouri and Ohio rivers join to form the third largest river system in the world. It is 6,236 kilometres (3,877 miles) long.

Glossary

Arctic Circle imaginary line that circles the Earth near the North Pole

Aztecs people who lived in Mexico about 500 years ago

border dividing line between one country and another

canal large man-made channel, filled with water, that ships and boats travel through

capital city city where government leaders work

climate type of weather a place has

desert hot, dry place with very little rain

freshwater water that is not salty

lumberjack someone who cuts down trees and saws them into logs

maple syrup sweet, thick liquid that can be eaten

national park area of wild land protected by the government

Native Americans first people to live in North America

parliament group of people who make the laws of their country

plains large, flat areas of land

port town or city with a harbour, where ships come and go

range line of mountains that are connected to each other

sap sugary liquid inside a plant or tree

settlers people who come to live in a country

shallow not very deep

swamp very wet, muddy land

temple place built to worship a god or goddess

More books to read

My World of Geography: Lakes, Angela Royston
(Heinemann Library, 2004)

Watching Grizzly Bears in North America, Elizabeth Miles
(Heinemann Library, 2006)

We're from Mexico, Vic Parker (Heinemann Library, 2005)

Index